JAVA PROGRAMMING

LEARN HOW TO CODE WITH AN OBJECT-ORIENTED PROGRAM TO IMPROVE YOUR SOFTWARE ENGINEERING SKILLS. GET FAMILIAR WITH VIRTUAL MACHINE, JAVASCRIPT, AND MACHINE CODE

ALAN GRID

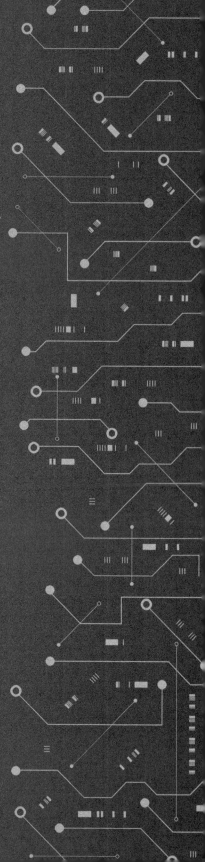

TABLE OF CONTENTS

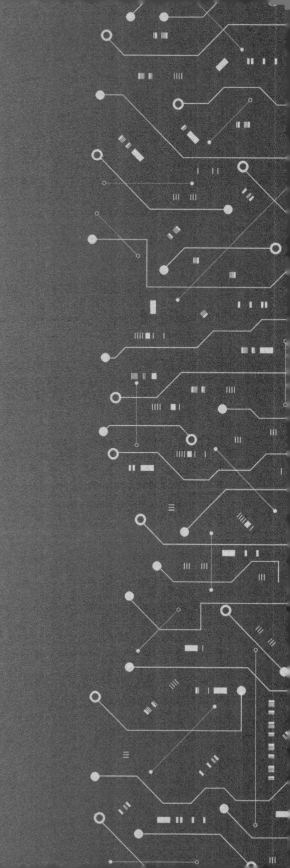

INTRODUCTION

Java is a widely-used programming language on the Web and in computing applications. It is a free download solution that allows users to access the latest versions and implement updates. This particular programming language is present in the majority of today's web applications and computing technologies. Java's scalable characteristics make it suitable for deployment in a wide range of applications, including apps for small electronic devices like cell phones and software solutions for large scale operations such as data centers. The growing preference for deploying Java is attributable to its robust functional features and sound security credentials.

Java is a programming language that is built by Sun Microsystems, which was later taken over by the Oracle Corporation. It is designed to run on any operating system that supports Java. This is what made the language so popular, because the developer just had to write the program once, and the program could then run on any operating system without the need for the programmer to change the code.

Most of the modern applications built around the world are made from the Java programming language. Most of the server-side and business logic components of major applications are built on the Java programming language.

During the entire course of this book, you will learn how to write programs such as the one above, and also learn advanced concepts that will enable you to start writing complete application programs.

Some of the design goals for Java are mentioned below:

- The language is intended to be written once and have the ability to be run on any operating system.

- The language should provide support for numerous software engineering principles.

Portability is an important factor. This is why Java has the ability to run on Windows, Linux, and the MacOS operating system.

Support for internationalization is very important.

Java is intended to be suitable for writing applications for both hosted and embedded systems.

Other design goals are discussed next:

Strong Type Checking

Java is a strong type language. Every variable that is defined needs to be attached to a data type.

You don't need to understand the complete program for now, but let's just have a quick look at 2 lines of the code.

```
1)      int i=5;
```

Here we are defining something known as a variable, which is used to hold a value. The value that can be stored depends on the data type. In this example, we are saying that 'i' is of the type 'int' or Integer, which is a numeric data value.

Array Bounds Checking

At runtime, Java will check whether the array has the required number of values defined. If one tries to access a value which is outside the bounds of the array, an exception will be thrown.

You don't need to understand the complete program for now, but let's just have a quick look at the following lines of the code.

```
1)      int[] array1 = new int[2];
```

Here we are declaring an array, which is a set of integer values. The value of '2' means that we can only store two values in the array.

```
2)      array1[0] = 1;

array1[1] = 2;

array1[2] = 3;
```

With this code, we can see that we are assigning 3 values to the array. When you run this program, you will get an error because the program will see that the array has gone out of its maximum allowable bounds of two. You will get the below error at runtime.

Exception in thread "main" java.lang. ArrayIndexOutOfBoundsException: 2

```
at HelloWorld.main(HelloWorld.java:8)
```

Why Java is important?

Next, Java has syntax and features that resemble other programming languages like C and C++. If you have any prior programming experience, you will find learning Java a breeze. Even if you are totally new to programming, you can rest assured that Java is designed to be a relatively easy language to learn. Most programmers find it easier to learn

Java than say, C or C++.

Java is also designed to be platform-independent. As mentioned earlier, Java code is compiled into bytecode first, which can be run on any machine that has the Java Virtual Machine.

Hence with Java, you can write the code once and run it anywhere you want.

Why Java?

Of course, one of the key reasons to use Java is its focus on Object-oriented programming.

Object-oriented programming, or "OOP" is a type of programming language model which allows the program's code to be organized around data, rather than functions and logic, which is known as procedural programming.

These "data clusters" are organized into things called "objects," hence the moniker of "object-oriented programming."

These objects are created by something called "classes," understood here in the traditional sense of how classes are: types of objects, allowing the programmer to "classify" them according to two major criteria: attributes and methods.

The attributes of a class are the raw data that will create the object: these are its descriptors, such as the values that it possesses, and other relevant data that will make up the object. The second criterion is the "method" of the object.

This "method" is the behavior, or the logical sequences contained within the class, describing how it interacts or can be interacted with natively

CHAPTER - 1
JAVA BASICS

O f course, one of the key reasons to use Java is its focus on Object-oriented programming. Object-oriented programming, or "OOP" is a type of programming language model which allows the program's code to be organized around data, rather than functions and logic, which is known as procedural programming.

These objects are created by something called "classes," understood here in the traditional sense of how classes are types of objects, allowing the programmer to "classify" them according to two major criteria: attributes and methods.

The attributes of a class are the raw data that will create the object: these are its descriptors, such as the values that it possesses, and other relevant data that will make up the object.

The second criterion is the "method" of the object.

In order to make this clearer, say that there is a class "Human." This "class" will have attributes such as height, weight, gender, and race. The "human" class can also have methods such as "run," "walk," "talk." These theoretical components make up the "human" class, a blueprint for an object.

Now that the class has been defined, the programmer, if they so wish, can create an object using the "human" class as a blueprint.

They can invoke the class "Human" and "populate" its attributes, giving it a specific height, weight, gender, and race. In addition, the object already has built-in functions such as "run," "walk," and "talk," so upon the creation of an object, let's say named "Mike" from the "Human" class, it already contains the functions to run, walk, and talk, without need for the programmer to code those specific functions again, as they are already "inherent" in the created object.

In a nutshell, that is what Object-oriented programming is meant to be: a way of programming that allows the programmer to draw on pre-defined classes so that it will be easier to describe them and use their internal, or built-in functions in order to operate them.

Assuming that the reader is not a total newbie to programming, and has been introduced to the world of programming using C or another procedural—heavy language, the next logical question would be: why even use object-oriented programming?

Well, one of its main advantages is that in the long run, it saves time.

Procedural programming is usually much quicker and more straightforward in simpler algorithms and programs; rather than having to construct and define a class, and create an object based on that class, all the programmer really has to do is to simply declare the necessary variables and write the functions, and create the algorithm in order to solve the problem that they need the code to address.

However, when it comes to more complex programs, needing more complex solutions, this is where object-oriented programming begins to shine, and this is where it starts to show its strength.

In a lot of programs, there will be times that there will be a number of "objects" or data clusters that have to be grouped together, and that the programmer will be treated in a certain way.

This is what "classes" are meant to address.

Instead of declaring a new set of variables per data cluster, they can simply draw on a pre-made "class" and create a new "object."

Let's see how this would work in practice.

If a programmer were to code a chess game in procedural fashion, then they would have to manually describe each and every piece, all sixteen pawns, four bishops and four knights, four rooks, two queens, and two kings. In addition, they will have to write the functions that allow each piece to move in its own separate way.

However, if the programmer makes use of object-oriented programming, instead of having to code sixteen pawns, four bishops, four knights, four rooks, two queens, two kings, they simply have to code six classes: one class to describe each piece on the board.

The programmer can now simply include the movement functions within each class, and have the attributes describe their position: whether they're white king's pawn, or black queen's pawn, these are all things that can be inserted through the "attributes" portion of the "pawn" class. Instead of thirty—two clusters of code, the programmer only has to do six.

Now it's much easier, much shorter, and also much more elegant.

Java tokens

Java tokens are the values that are smaller than other integers.

These numbers are going to fall between the value of -32768 and 32767.

The code that I have been using is not going to work for shorts, instead, I am going to need to use the short function so that I can make sure that the values are going to fall between the set limitations.

Large values are going to be stored inside of a double value along with floating-point values.

A double does not have to be used if I can use a floating-point. As I am storing a floating variable.

I am going to need to put a letter at the end of my value amount.

This value should be f because it is a floating-point number.

Keywords

In Java, the Boolean type refers to false or true values. J

Ava finds out if it is true or false using the reserved keywords. Therefore, a Boolean expression type will assume one of these values.

An example to demonstrate include:

There are a few things to note about this program.

First, the println(), displays a boolean value. Secondly, the boolean values control the flow of an if statement.

You don't need to go a long way in writing the boolean type this way: if (b == true)

The result shown by the operator, such as < is boolean. It is one of the reasons why we have the expression 11 > 8 showing the value true.

In addition, the other pair of parentheses near the 11 > 8 is important since plus comes before the >.

Identifiers

The top layer of the diagram above is for the identifier or name.

This top layer is the name you give to a class. The name should specifically identify and also describe the type of object as seen or experienced by the user.

In simple terms, the name or identifier should identify the class.

Operators

Java has an extensive list of operator environment.

If you are wondering what an operator is, you can look at it as a symbol that conveys a specific message to the compiler to carry out a logical or mathematical operation. In Java, you will interact with four classes of operators.

The four classes include:

- Logical operator

- Bitwise operator

- Relational operator

- Arithmetic operator

Like other computer languages, Java has a defined list of additional operators to take care of certain specific scenarios.

When it comes to learning JAVA programming language, or any programming language for that matter, there are five basic concepts you must understand before you get started.

These five basic concepts include:

- Variables

- Data Structures

- Control Structures

- Syntax

- Tools

Each of these concepts will be thoroughly explained on a beginner's level to ensure that they are understood.

Separators

They are not suitable for high-level abstraction: note that a lot of these programs make use of low-level constructs which are primarily used for low-level abstraction.

The usual approach with these programming languages is that they focus on the machine—how to make a computer do something rather than how these functions can help solve the issues of a user.

These languages deal with the minute details, which is already beyond the scope of high-level abstraction, which is the more common approach that we see today.

In low-level abstraction, data structures and algorithms are taken separately, whereas these are taken as a whole in high-level abstraction.

Literals

When it comes to literals in Java, we mean the fixed values which appear in the form in which human beings can read. We can say the number 200 is literal. Most of the time, literals can be constants.

Literals are important in a program. In fact, most Java programs use literals. Some of the programs we have already discussed in this book use literals.

Literals in Java can fall on various primitive data types.

The manner in which every literal is shown is determined by its type. Like it was mentioned some time back, we enclose character constants in single quotes such as 'c' and '%.'

We define literals in integers without involving the fractional part. For instance, 12 and -30 are integer literals. A floating-point literal should contain the decimal point plus the fractional part. 12.389 is a floating literal.

Java further permits for one to apply the scientific notation for the floating-point literals.

Integer literals contain int value, and anyone can initialize them with a variable of short, byte, and char.

Comments

When this occurs, we call the grey's comments. In the running stages of the program, the grey's (comments) are moot.

This is to means that you can use the comment feature to state or explain what the code you are creating wants to achieve.

You can achieve this by typing two slashes and then the comment. Here is a sample.

//Place your single line comment here

You can have more than one comment line by doing either of the following:

```
//We are going to

//spread the comments into two
```

Or

```
/*
```

This comment spreads over two lines

```
*/
```

If you look at the comment above, you will notice that it starts with /* but ends with */

Additionally, if you look at the previous image (figure 8, you will notice that there are comments that begin with a single forward slash and two asterisks (/**), but end with one asterisk and one forwards slash; this is called a Javadoc comment.

CHAPTER - 2

VARIABLES

What are variables?

A variable, on the other hand, is an "object" that contains a specific data type and it's assigned or received value. It is called a variable because the value contained can change according to how it is used in the code, how the coder can declare its value, or even how the user of the program chooses to interact with it. A variable, in short, is a storage unit for a data type. Having access to variables allow programmers to conveniently label and call stored values at hand.

Types of variables in Java

Java requires the programmer to use declaration statements, lines of code used to declare variables and define them by specifying the particular data type and name. Java has a specific way of treating variables, by defining variables as containers that contain a certain type and value of information, unlike some languages such as python, which only requires a declaration of a variable, and the variable can dynamically change its type; Java variables are static, which retain their type once declared.

```
Int number = 20;

Boolean completed = true;

String hello = "Hello World!"
```

The syntax in declaring is seen in the previous examples, with the type of the variable coming first, then the name of the variable, then the value. Note as well that the declaration statement can be composed of multiple declarations in one line, as in the following example:

Int number = 20, Boolean completed = true, string hello = "Hello World!";

Java variables can be declared without any value at the start; in cases such as these, Java chooses to declare these variables with a particular default value, for example:

```
Byte a;

Short num;

Boolean answer;
```

Will result in the values 0, 0, and false, respectively. A more complete list of default values is as follows: the byte, short, int, and long data types will all result in a default value of 0, while the float and double data types will have a default 0.0 value, the char data type will result in 'u\0000' value, a string or any other object will have a null default value, and all Booleans will begin with a false default value.

In Java, variables are static when declared, meaning that the programmer must define the data type that the variable will be containing. To illustrate, if we wish to use a variable num to store a number, we would first have to declare the variable: "int num," before we can assign a value, such as "num = 10."

The process above is usually known as and referred to as an "assignment statement," where a value is assigned to the variable as declared by the programmer. However, one prominent thing about how Java, and in fact how most programming languages, works is that in the assignment statement, such as in our example of num = 10, the actual value stored is the one on the right side of the equals sign, the value of 10, and num is just the "marker" to call that stored value. This is why there are many Java programmers that tend to prefer the jargon of "getting" a value rather than "assigning," though for the most part, they may be employed interchangeably, and outside of some rare scenario, function mostly the same way.

Note, however, that once values have been assigned to variables, functions need to be carried out in order for the data inside that variable to change its data type.

Naming a variable

Creating variables is an easy task, especially given how Java programmers tend to create and name them after the data type or the purpose of what the variable will store. However, there are a few rules when it comes to naming these variables, else Java will not recognize it, and an error message will result. The main restrictions around variable names are that it should not begin with a special character, such as an underscore or a number. However, variable names can consist of characters such as letters and numbers, and even an underscore, provided that the underscore is not placed at the start. No other characters may be used, such as the # or even $, as these special characters have different uses in Java, and thus will not be recognized in a variable name.

While those are the major rules, here are some tips when it comes to naming variables. The variable name should be descriptive, as in longer codes it may be difficult to recall just what "x" is for. Having a variable name such as "count" or "output" is much easier to recall as compared to having a generic "x" or "y" and will help in avoiding confusion. In addition to being descriptive, variables will also be easier to use if their names are kept fairly short. While having a variable name such as banking information account records is very descriptive, typing it repeatedly as needed in the program will get exhausting, and having longer variable names increase the chances of typographical errors, which will lead to bugs in the code, resulting in a run - time error or the code not working as intended, or working, but introducing bugs along the way. Note as well that it has always been a practice for Java variables to be written in all lower—case letters, and while there is no restriction on capitalization, keeping things in lowercase simplifies things, as a missed capitalization may result in the variable not being recognized, as Java reads an upper—case letter as an entirely different character versus a lower—case letter.

Java primitive types

Method Naming Conventions

We shall revisit the naming conventions in Java since you will be using member methods. Methods in Java programming perform operations, they also receive any argument provided by a caller, and it can also return a result of an operation to a caller. Here's the syntax for declaring a method:

```
[Access Control Modifier] Return Type
methodName ([set of parameters]) {
```

```
    // body of the method

    ......

}
```

Here are a few rules to remember when you make the names for the methods that you will write. Method names are always verbs or more specifically verb phrases (which means you can use multiple words to name them). The first word of the method name should all be in lower case letters, while the rest of the words should follow a camel case format. Here is an example:

```
writeMethodNamesThisWay( )
```

Now, you should remember that verbs are used for method names, and they indicate an action while nouns are used for variable names, and they denote a certain attribute.

Following the syntax for declaring a method and following the name conventions for this Java construct, here's a sample code that can be used to compute the area of a circle.

```
public double computeCircleArea() {
```

```
return radius * radius * Math.PI;

}
```

Using Constructors in Your Code

We'll just go over some additional details as they relate to object-oriented programming. As stated earlier, a constructor will look like a method, and you can certainly think of it and treat it like a special kind of method in Java programming.

However, a constructor will still be different from a method in several ways. The name of a constructor will be the same as the class name. Use the keyword or operator "new" to create a new instance of the constructor and also to initialize it. Here's an example using the class "Employee" and a variety of ways to initialize it in your code:

```
Employee payrate1 = new Employee( );

Employee payrate2 = new Employee(2.0);

Employee payrate3 = new Employee(3.0,
"regular");
```

A constructor will also implicitly return void—that simply means it doesn't have a return type. You can't put a return statement inside the body of a constructor since it will be flagged by compilers as an error. The only way you can invoke a constructor is via the use of the "new" statement. We have already given you several ways how you can invoke constructors in the samples above.

One final difference is that constructors can't be inherited. Let's go back to the examples provided above—the first line includes "Employee( );"—that is called a default constructor. As you can see, it has no parameters whatsoever. The job of a default constructor is to simply initialize the member variables to a specific default value. In the example above, the member variable payrate1 was initialized to its default pay rate and employee status.

Can constructors be overloaded too? Yes, they can. Constructors behave like methods too, so that means you can overload a constructor just the same way you overload a method. Here are a few examples of how you can overload a constructor. We use the Employee class and overload it using different parameters.

```
Employee( )

Employee(int r)

Employee(int r, String b)
```

How to initialize a variable

Now that we know how to declare variables, and we know the various types of variables that are available to us, the next thing to do is to learn how to make use of these variables, in something called "expressions." Expressions are the most used building blocks of a Java program, generally meant to produce a new value as a result, though in some cases, expressions are used to assign a new value to a variable. Generally, expressions are made up of things such as values, variables, operators, and method calls. There are also some expressions that produce no result, but rather affect another variable. One example would be an expression that changes the value of a variable based on an operation: there is no new value output, and there is no true "assignment" of a new value, but rather there is what is called a side effect that results in a changed variable value.

The "Hello World" printing program, we introduced raw values into the print function, also known as "hard coding" the output. However, at this point, we should try to incorporate what we have learned about variables. Variables operate much the same way as raw values, as they simply reference a previously stored value by the computer, and as such, the programmer can just use the variable name instead of the value. In order to demonstrate this, let us remember the previous "Hello World" program:

```
print ("Hello World") ;

input ("\n\nPlease press the return key to close
this window.") ;
```

Now, instead of hard—coding the "Hello World" string, we can simply declare it into a variable and have the program output that variable. This should end up looking as:

```
String = "Hello World" ;

print(string) ;

input ("\n\nPlease press the return key to close
this window.") ;
```

This should come out with the same result as the previous program, looking something similar to:

Hello World

Please press the return key to close this window.

CHAPTER - 3
JAVA BASICS

Java Development Kit

The JDK provides the tools needed to build, test, and monitor robust Java-anchored applications. It allows developers to access software components and compile applications during Java programming operations. For example, a developer needs a JDK-powered environment to be able to write applets or implement methods.

Since the JDK more or less performs the operations of a Software Development Kit (SDK), one could easily confuse the scope and operations of the two items. Whereas the JDK is specific to the Java programming language, an SDK has broader applicability. But a JDK still operates as a component of an SDK in a program development environment. This means that a developer would still need an SDK to provide certain tools with broader operational characteristics and that are not available within the JDK domain. Developer documentation and debugging utilities, as well as application servers, are some of the crucial tools that SDK supplies to a Java programming environment.

The scope of JDK deployment depends on the nature of the tasks at hand, the supported versions, and the Java edition that is in use. For example, the Java Platform, Standard Edition (Java SE) Development Kit is designed for use with the Java Standard Edition. The Java Platform, Enterprise Edition (Java EE), and the Java Platform, Macro Edition (Java ME), are the other major subsets of the JDK. Details of each of these Java editions are described in detail in the subtopics below. The JDK has been a free platform since 2007, when it was uploaded to the OpenJDK portal. Its open-source status facilitates collaborations and allows communities of software developers to clone, hack, or contribute ideas for advancements and upgrades.

Java SE

The Java SE powers a wide variety of desktop and server applications. It supports the testing and deployment of the Java programming language within the development environment of these applications. Some of the documentations associated with the recent releases of Java SE include an advanced management console feature and a revamped set of Java deployment rules. Java

SE 13.0.1 is the latest JDK version for the Java SE platform at the time of writing this book.

The Java SE SDK is equipped with the core JRE capabilities alongside a portfolio of tools, class libraries, and implementation technologies that are designed for use in the development of desktop applications. These tools range from simple objects and types for Java program implementations to advanced class parameters that are suited for building applications with networking capabilities and impenetrable security characteristics. Java programmers can also apply this particular JDK on the development of Java applications used to simplify access to databases or to enhance GUI properties.

Java EE

The Java EE platform is an open-source product that is developed through the collaborative efforts of members of the Java community worldwide. Java EE is closely related to the Java SE because the former is built on top of the latter. This particular software is integrated with transformative innovations that are designed for use in enterprise solutions. The features and advancements that are introduced in new releases often reflect the inputs, requirements, and requests of members of the Java community. The Java EE actually offers more than twenty implementations that are compliant with Java programming.

The Java EE SDK is meant for use in the construction of applications for large-scale operations. Just as its name suggests, this particular Java SDK was created to provide support for enterprise software solutions. The JDK features a powerful API and runtime properties that Java programmers require to build applications with scalable and networkable functionalities. Developers in need of developing multi-tiered applications could find this JDK useful as well.

The Java EE 8 is the latest release at the time of writing this book. Java EE's revised design provides enhanced technologies for enterprise solutions as well as modernized applications for security and management purposes. The release features several advancements that included greater REST API capabilities provided through the Client, JSON Binding, Servlet, and Security APIs. This version also features the Date and Time API as well as the Streams API, according to information published in the Oracle Corporate website as of December 2019.

Java ME

The Java ME platform deploys simplicity, portability, and dynamism to provide a versatile environment for building applications for small gadgets and devices. Java ME is known for having an outstanding application development environment, thanks to its interactive and user-friendly navigation interfaces, as well as built-in capabilities for implementing networking concepts. It is largely associated with the Internet of Things (IoT) and is useful when building applications designed for built-in technologies or connected devices that could be used to invent or implement futuristic concepts. Java ME's portability and runtime attributes make it suitable for use in software applications for wearable gadgets, cell phones, cameras, sensors, and printers, among other items and equipment.

The Java ME SDK is equipped with the requisite tools meant for use within an independent environment when developing software applications, testing functionalities, and implementing device simulations. According to information published in the Oracle Corporate website as of 2019, this JDK is well suited for accommodating "the Connected Limited Device Configuration (CLDC)" technology alongside "the Connected Device Configuration (CDC)" functionality. This results in a single and versatile environment for developing applications.

There are several other Java ME solutions that support the deployment of the Java programming language in applications. Java ME Embedded provides a runtime environment integrating IoT capabilities in devices, while the Java ME embedded client facilitates the construction of software solutions that run and optimize the functionality of built-in programs. Java for Mobile makes use of the CLDC and the stack of Java ME developer tools to create innovative features for mobile devices.

Java Runtime Environment

Remember that there are certain conditions that must prevail for Java applications to run efficiently. The JRE contains the ingredients responsible for creating these requisite conditions. This includes the JVM and its corresponding files and class attributes. Although JRE operates as a component of the JDK, it is capable of operating independently, especially if the tasks are limited to run rather than build application instructions.

The JRE lends important operational properties to different programs in the Java programming ecosystem. For example, a program is considered self-contained if it runs an independent JRE within it. This means that a program does not depend on other programs to access the JRE. This independence makes it possible for a program to achieve compatibility with different OS platforms.

Java Virtual Machine

The JVM operates as a specification for implementing Java in computer programs. It is the driving force behind the platform-independence characteristics of the Java language. This status is accentuated by JVM's status as a program that is executed by other programs. The programs written to interact with and execute the JVM see it as a machine. It is for this reason that similar sets, libraries, and interfaces are used to write Java programs to be able to match every single JVM implementation to a particular

OS. This facilitates the translation or interpretation of Java programs into runtime instructions in the local OS, and thereby eliminating the need for platform dependence in Java programming.

As a developer, you must be wary of the vulnerability your development environment and applications have to cyber attacks and other threats. The JVM provides enhanced security features that protect you from such threats. The solid security foundation is attributable to its built-in syntax and structure limitations that reside in the operational codes of class files. But this does not translate to limitations on the scope of class files that the JVM can accommodate. The JVM actually accepts a variety of class files so long as they can be validated to be safe and secure. Therefore, the JVM is a viable complementary alternative for developing software in other programming languages.

The JVM is often included as a ported feature in a wide variety of software applications and hardware installations. It is implemented through algorithms that are determined by Oracle or any other provider. As such, the JVM provides an open implementation platform. The JVM actually contains the runtime instance as the core property that anchors its command operations. For example, the creation of a JVM instance simply involves writing an instruction in the command prompt that, in turn, runs the class properties of Java.

A Java programmer needs to be familiar with the key areas of JVM, such as the classloader and the data section for runtime operations as well as the engine that is responsible for executing programs. There are also performance-related components, such as the garbage collector and the heap dimension tool, that are equally important to the deployment of the JVM. There is a close affiliation between the JVM and bytecodes.

Bytecodes

Bytecodes are essentially JVM commands that are contained in a class file alongside other information that include the symbol table. They operate as background language programs responsible for facilitating the interpretation and execution of JVM operations. Bytecodes are actually the substitutes for native codes because Java does not provide the latter. The structure of the JVM register is such that it contains methods which, in turn, accommodate bytecode streams—that is, sets of instructions for the JVM. In other words, each Java class has methods within it, and the class file loading process executes a single bytecode stream for any given method. The activation of a method automatically triggers a bytecode the moment a program begins to run.

The other important feature of bytecodes is the Just-in-time (JIT) compiler that operates during the runtime operations for compiling codes that can be executed. The feature actually exists as a HotSpot JIT compiler within the JVM ecosystem. It executes codes concurrently with the Java runtime operations because it has the ability to perform at optimized levels and the flexibility to scale and accommodate growing traffic of instructions. Previously, the JIT compiler required frequent tuning to rid it of redundant programs and refresh its memory. Tuning was a necessary procedure that ensured the JIT compiler delivered optimum performance. However, the frequent upgrades in the newer versions of Java gradually introduced automated memory refreshing mechanisms that eliminated the need for regular tuning.

Bytecodes can be either primitive types, flexible types, or stack-based. According to Venners (1996), there are seven parameters of primitive data, including byte, char, double, float, int, long, and short. The boolean parameter is also a widely used primitive type, taking the tally to eight. Each of the eight parameters is meant to help developers deploy variables that can be acted upon by the bytecodes. Bytecode streams actually express these parameters of the primitive types in the form of operands. This ends up designating the larger and more powerful parameters to the higher levels of the bytes' hierarchy, with the smaller ones occupying the lower levels of the hierarchy in a descending order.

Java opcodes are similarly crucial components of

the primitive types, thanks to their role of classifying operands. This role ensures that operands retain their state, thereby eliminating the need for an operand identification interface in the JVM. The JVM is able to speed up processes because it is capable of multitasking while accommodating multiple opcodes that deliver domicile variables into stacks. Opcodes are also useful for processing and defining the value parameters for stack-based bytecodes. According to Venners (1996), this could be an implicit constant value, an operand value, or a value derived from a constant pool.

CHAPTER - 4
JAVA ENVIRONMENT

Writing Programs in Editors

To write programs, you use a simple editor such as Notepad, or you can use a full-fledged Integrated Development Environment (IDE). Below is a list of some of the most popular IDE's that are available for Java and some of their relevant features.

Eclipse

This IDE has been around for quite a long time and is very popular and widely used amongst the Java development community. Some of the core features of the IDE are:

- It's free and open source. Hence there are many developers who keep contributing to the IDE.

- It can be used to develop applications in other languages such as C++, Ruby, HTML5, and PHP.

- It has a rich client platform.

- It provides the ability of refactoring code.

- It helps in code completion.

- It has a wide variety of extensions and plugins.

- It also has support for most source code version control systems.

IntelliJ IDEA

This is another popular IDE used by the Java development community. Some of the core features of this IDE are:

- The community edition is free and open source.

- The paid edition provides many more features and allows developers to build enterprise applications with the Java Enterprise Edition.

- It provides the ability of refactoring code.

- It helps in code completion.

- It has a wide variety of extensions and plugins.

- It also has support for most source code version control systems.

Netbeans

NetBeans is a highly recommended IDE for beginners in Java language. It is a powerful and fast IDE that supports all Java platforms as well as mobile applications. It runs on a variety of platforms such as Windows, Linux, Mac OS X, and Solaris. It also provides support for languages such as HTML5, C/C++, and PHP.

The Upsides of Java

Java epitomizes simplicity in programming, thanks to its user-friendly interface for learning, writing, deployment, and implementation.

- Java's core architecture is designed to facilitate ease of integration and convenience of use within the development environment.

- Java is platform-independent and readily portable, making it suitable for multitasking and use across software applications.

- The object-oriented characteristics of Java support the creation of programs with standard features and codes that can be redeployed.

- Java's networking capabilities make it easier for programmers to create software solutions for shared computing environments.

- The close relationship between Java, the C++, and the C languages makes it easier for anyone with knowledge of the other two languages to learn Java.

- Java's automated garbage collection provides continuous memory protection, making it convenient for programmers to eliminate security vulnerabilities while writing codes.

- Java's architecture is flexible for the implementation of multithreading programs.

- Java is readily reusable, thanks to the ability to redeploy classes using the interface or inheritance features.

The Downsides of Java

- Since Java is not a native application, it runs at lower speeds compared to other programming languages.

- Java may also lack consistency in the processing and displaying of graphics. For example, the ordinary appearance of the graphical user interface (GUI) in Java-based applications is quite different and of lower standards compared the GUI output of native software applications.

- Java's garbage collection, a feature that manages memory efficiency, may interfere with speed and performance whenever it runs as a background application.

CHAPTER - 5

OBJECTS AND CLASSES

Finally, we are going to look at classes and objects;

An object in Java has got to have a state, which will be stored in a field and a behavior, indicated by a method.

A class is a sort of map, a blueprint if you like, from which an object is created. This is what a class looks like:

```java
public class Dog {

    String breed;

    int ageC;

    String color;

    void whining() {
```

```
    }

    void sleeping() {

    }

}
```

A class may have any of these variable types:

- Local—defined within a constructor, block, or method. The variable is declared and then initialized inside a method and destroyed once the method has ended.

- Instance—defined in a class but are outside a method. Initialized when instantiation of the class happens and can be accessed from inside any constructor, block, or method of the class.

- Class—declared inside the class, uses the static keyword, and are outside any method.

Classes can have multiple methods, as many as required to access all the different kinds of values in the method. In our example above, we had three methods—barking(), whining(), and sleeping().

Constructors

Every class will have a constructor; if you omit it, a default one will be built by the compiler. When you create a new object, at least one constructor must be invoked. As a rule, the name of a constructor must be the same as that of the class, and there can be as many constructors as a class requires.

This is what a constructor looks like:

```java
public class Puppy {

public Puppy() {

}

public Puppy(String name) {

    // This constructor has a single parameter, name.

}

}
```

Creating Objects

We already know that a class is a kind of blueprint to create objects from, so it goes without saying that the object is created from the class. For a new object to be created, we need the new keyword.

These are the three steps needed to create an object from a class:

Declaration—A variable must be declared with a name and the object type

Instantiation—The new keyword is used for creating the object

Initialization—The constructor is called, and this initializes the object.

The next example shows how objects are created:

```java
public class Puppy {

public Puppy(String name) {

// This constructor contains a single parameter called name.

System.out.println("Passed Name is :" + name );

}

public static void main(String []args) {

// The next statement will create an object called myPuppy

Puppy myPuppy = new Puppy( "fluffy" );

}

}
```

Run this and see what happens.

Accessing Instance Variables and Methods

Objects can be used when we want to access instance variables and methods; this example shows how we access an instance variable:

```
/* First we create the object */

ObjectReference = new Constructor();

/* Now we call our variable, like this */

ObjectReference.variableName;

/* Now a class method is called, like this */

ObjectReference.MethodName();
```

Next, we can see the instance variables and methods in a class are accessed:

```
public class Puppy {

int PuppyAge;

public Puppy(String name) {

// This constructor contains a single parameter called name.

System.out.println("Name chosen is :" + name );
```

```java
}
public void setAge(int age) {

PuppyAge = age;

}
public int getAge() {

System.out.println("Puppy's age is :" + PuppyAge
);

return PuppyAge;

}
public static void main(String[] args) {

/* Object creation */

Puppy myPuppy = new Puppy( "fluffy" );

/* Now we call the class method to set the
Puppy's age */

myPuppy.setAge(2);

/* Next, we call another class method to get the
Puppy's age */

myPuppy.getAge();

/* We access instance variable in this way */

System.out.println("Variable Value :" + myPuppy.
PuppyAge );
```

```
}

}
```

Run this and see what happens.

Import Statements

One important thing to remember is that paths must be fully qualified, and that includes the names of the class and the package. If not, the compiler will struggle to load the source code and the classes. To qualify a path, we need to use import statements and, in this example, we see how a compiler loads the requested classes into the directory we specify:

```
import java.io.*;
```

Next, we need two classes created, one called Employee and one called EmployeeTest. We use the following code to do this—keep in mind that Employee is the name of the class, and it is a public class. Do this and then save the file, calling it Employee.java.

Also note that we have four instance variables here—age, name, designation, and salary, along with one constructor that has been explicitly defined and that takes a parameter:

```java
public class Employee {

String name;

int age;

String designation;

double salary;

// This is the constructor of the class called Employee

public Employee(String name) {

this.name = name;

}

// We assign the age of the Employee to the variable called age.

public void empAge(int empAge) {

age = empAge;

}

/* We assign the designation to the variable called designation.*/

public void empDesignation(String empDesig) {

designation = empDesig;

}
```

```java
/* We assign the salary to the variable called salary.*/

public void empSalary(double empSalary) {

salary = empSalary;

}

/* Print the Employee details */

public void printEmployee() {

System.out.println("Name:"+ name );

System.out.println("Age:" + age );

System.out.println("Designation:" + designation );

System.out.println("Salary:" + salary);

}

}
```

Code processing begins with a main method, so you need to ensure that your code has a main method, and we need to create some objects. We will start by creating a class called EmployeeTest, and this will create a couple of instances of the class called Employee. The methods for each object must be invoked so that the values may be assigned to the variables. Save this code in EmployeeTest:

```java
public class EmployeeTest {

public static void main(String args[]) {

/* Create two objects by using constructor */

Employee empOne = new Employee("Bobby Bucket");

Employee empTwo = new Employee("Shelley Mary");

// Invoke the methods for each of the objects we created

empOne.empAge(28);

empOne.empDesignation("Senior        Software Developer");

empOne.empSalary(1500);

empOne.printEmployee();

empTwo.empAge(22);

empTwo.empDesignation("Software Developer");

empTwo.empSalary(850);

empTwo.printEmployee();

}

}
```

Now the classes need to be compiled, and EmployeeTest run; do this and see what you get.

You should see this:

Output

C:\> javac Employee.java

C:\> javac EmployeeTest.java

C:\> java EmployeeTest

Name: Bobby Bucket

Age:28

Designation: Senior Software Developer

Salary:1850.000

Name: Shelley Mary

Age:22

Designation: Software Developer

Salary:850.00

CHAPTER - 6

PROPER WORKING CODE EXAMPLES

Traditionally, everyone's first program prints, "Hello World." This first program demonstrates how to create, save, and run a program. It also shows the basic structure used in all Java programs.

Here's a screenshot of the window created by the Hello World program:

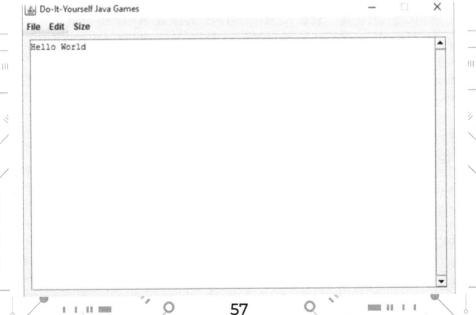

Lesson 1—Java Projects and Packages

Programs are first organized by Java projects, then by packages within the Java projects. You'll create a Java project for each program in this book.

Packages hold program files that are usually used together. Because the programs in this book will be small, most of the Java projects you create will have only one package.

In this lesson, you'll create one Java project and one package for your first program.

Try It

Create your first Java project, called Hello World:

1. If Eclipse is no longer open:

- Double-click the Eclipse shortcut you created on your desktop.

- Click OK to use your Java work folder as your workspace.

2. Right-click in the Package Explorer pane and choose New/Java Project.

3. Name the Java project Hello World, and select Use Default JRE if it is 1.7 or higher, then click next, as shown in the image below. If the default JRE is less than 1.7, select the option to Use an execution environment JRE of 1.7 or higher.

Name the project
Use Default JRE (1.7 or higher)

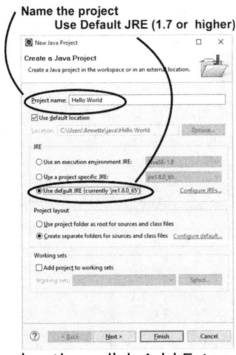

4. Click Libraries, then click Add External JARs..., as shown in the image below.

Libraries —— **Add External JAR**

5. Browse to and select DIYJava.jar, which you installed in your Java work folder, and click Open.

6. Click Finish.

The Package Explorer pane now lists one project (Hello World) with the added JAR file (DIYJava.jar), as shown in this image:

Create a package for your Hello World program in the Hello World project:

1. Right-click on the Hello World project and choose New/Package.

2. Name the package _____._____. helloworld, as shown in the image below. Use your own name as part of the package name. I used annette.godtland.helloworld for my package name.

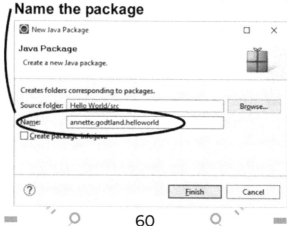

Name the package

3. Click Finish.

The Package Explorer pane now shows the package you created in your Hello World project, as shown in this image:

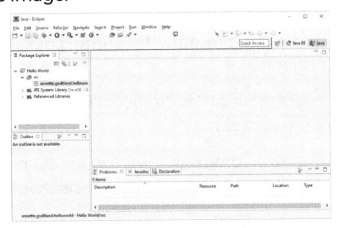

Key Points and More

Right-click in the Package Explorer pane to create Java projects and packages.

- Create a different Java project for each program.

- Eclipse will create a folder on your computer named the same as the Java project. Give your Java project a name you want for the folder on your computer.

- You now have a folder called Hello World in your Java work folder.

- For example, capitalize the first letter of each word and put a space between each word like the Hello World project.

- Add DIYJava.jar to the Java projects you create

with the help of this book.

- DIYJava.jar is an external JAR file.

- DIYJava.jar makes it easy to write programs that print text to a window.

- Organize your program files into packages in Java projects.

- Put program files that are usually used together into one package.

- Because your programs will be small, most of your programs will have only one package.

- Package name rules:

- Make your package name different from anyone else's package names. Java programmers traditionally use their name or business name as the first part of their package name.

- Use all lowercase letters with no spaces.

- Use periods between different categories in the package name. For example, if the package name identifies who created the package and what the package will be used for, put a period between the creator and its purpose.

- Make sure when you create the Java Projects in this book that you select the option to Use an execution environment JRE of JavaSE-1.7 or higher. Once you select this option for creating a project, Eclipse will default to that option for all future Java Projects.

- Java projects are for Eclipse; packages are for Java. Because you're using Eclipse, you'll use both Java projects and packages. If you were to create Java programs without Eclipse, you would probably use only packages.

Lesson 2—Classes, Superclasses, and Programs

Java programs are made from one or more classes. Classes contain the actual program code: the instructions that, when run in sequence, perform the desired task.

Every class must name some other class as its superclass. For example, programs intended to run in a window must name some type of window class as its superclass.

In this lesson, you'll create your first class: a program that runs in a DIYWindow.

Try It

Create your first class using the DIYWindow class as its superclass:

1. Right-click on your package in the Package Explorer pane and choose New / Class.

2. Enter HelloWorld for the class name, as shown in the image below. (Hint: there's no space between "Hello" and "World.")

3. Click Browse for Superclass.

4. Enter "diy" for the type, select DIYWindow, as shown in the image below, and click OK.

5. Which method stubs would you like to create? Select these options, as shown in the image below:

a. Public static void main (String[] args).

b. Constructors from superclass.

c. It doesn't matter if the third option, Inherit abstract methods, is selected or not.

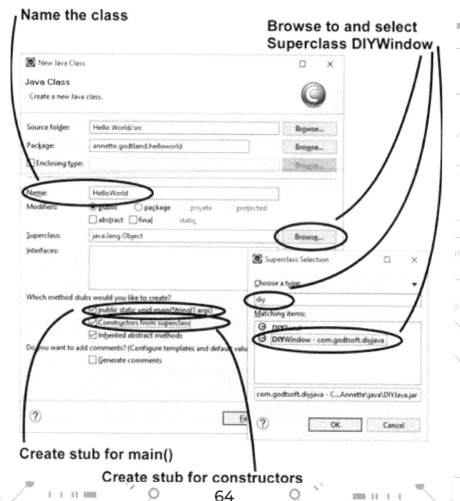

Name the class

Browse to and select Superclass DIYWindow

Create stub for main()

Create stub for constructors

6. Click Finish to create the class.

Eclipse will create code for a HelloWorld class that looks like the following listing.

You may find it easier to read the code listings in this book if you set your e-reader to a smaller font to minimize word wrapping.

Listing 1-1, from HelloWorld.java

```java
package annette.godtland.helloworld;

import com.godtsoft.diyjava.DIYWindow;

public class HelloWorld extends DIYWindow {

  public HelloWorld() {

    // TODO Auto-generated constructor stub

  }

  public static void main(String[] args) {

    // TODO Auto-generated method stub

  }

}
```

Eclipse adds comment code you don't need. Comments are lines that begin with // or groups of lines that begin with /* and end with */.

1. Remove the automatically-generated comment

lines from this class, where it says (Code was removed from here.) in the following listing.

Listing 1-2, from HelloWorld.java

```
package annette.godtland.helloworld;

import com.godtsoft.diyjava.DIYWindow;

public class HelloWorld extends DIYWindow {

  public HelloWorld() {


(Code was removed from here.)

  }

  public static void main(String[] args) {


(Code was removed from here.)

  }

}
```

Remove the automatically-generated comments from the program code for every class you create for this book. You'll add your own comments in later lessons.

Click any Completed listing link to see how to complete the code. However, you'll learn more if you try to complete the code yourself before you look up the answer.

The block of code that starts as a public static void main is called the main() method. The block of code that starts as public HelloWorld() is called the constructor.

Now, add your first lines of code:

1. Add code to the constructor and main() method exactly as shown here. Changes to make to code are always shown bold in the listings.

Listing 1-3, from HelloWorld.java

```
package annette.godtland.helloworld;

import com.godtsoft.diyjava.DIYWindow;

public class HelloWorld extends DIYWindow {

  public HelloWorld() {

print("Hello World");

  }

  public static void main(String[] args) {

new HelloWorld();

  }

}
```

1. Press Ctrl-S to save the program.

2. Click the Run button, as shown in this image, to run the program:

What happened?

A window should open that displays "Hello World," as shown in this image:

1. What would you have to change in your class to make it say hello to you?

Listing 1-4, from HelloWorld.java

```
...

public HelloWorld() {

  print("Hello

  _____

");

}

...
```

1. Save the program and run it.

What happens if you make a mistake?

1. Type the word "print" incorrectly and save the program.

Listing 1-5, from HelloWorld.java

```
...

public HelloWorld() {

  print

ttt

("Hello Annette");
```

```
}

...
```

What happened?

Many error indicators appear, as shown in this image:

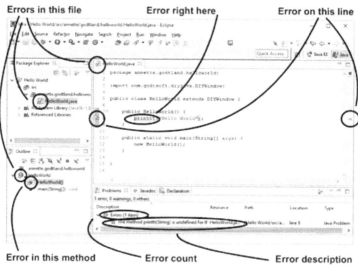

Errors in this file   Error right here   Error on this line

Error in this method   Error count   Error description

1. Double-click the Error count in the Problems pane of Eclipse to see the list of errors found.

2. Double-click on the Error description in the Problems pane to move your cursor to the line with the error.

3. Rest your cursor on the actual error (where it says Error right here in the above image). Eclipse will list ways to fix the problem, as shown in the image below. This feature of Eclipse is called Quick Fix.

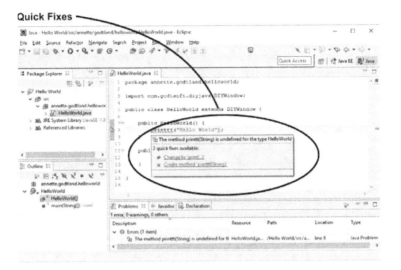

4. Click the quick fix called Change to "print(...)."

That action will fix the error for you.

1. Save changes.

All error indicators should disappear.

Now, print more:

1. Change the code to make your program say this:

Hello, earthling.

Take me to your leader.

Listing 1-6, from HelloWorld.java

```
...

public HelloWorld() {

print
```

```
("_____");

    print("_____");

}

...
```

Throughout the lessons, unless there are syntax errors, save changes, and run the program after every code change.

Did it print the correct lines? If not, fix the code and try again.

1. What do you think you would have to print to put a blank line between the two sentences, as shown below. (Hint: you want nothing printed on that line.)

Hello, earthling.

Take me to your leader.

Listing 1-7, from HelloWorld.java

```
    ...

  public HelloWorld() {

    print("Hello, earthling.");

print(___);

    print("Take me to your leader.");
```

```
}

...
```

Key Points and More

- Java programs are made up of classes. Every program requires a main() method in one of its classes.

o The main() method must be written as public static void main(String[] args). Later lessons will explain what all those words mean.

- Multiple classes are often used together to create one program. However, most of the programs in this book will be made of only one class.

- Every class must have a superclass. Any class can be used as a superclass. You'll create your own superclass in a later lesson.

- Classes with the same superclass are considered to be of the same type. For example, the main class you create for every program in this book will use the DIYWindow class as its superclass. So every program in this book will be a type of DIYWindow.

- To create classes, right-click in the Package Explorer pane.

o Class names can contain numbers, letters,

dollar signs, and underscores. Dollar signs and underscores are usually not used.

o Blanks or periods aren't allowed in class names.

o Class names cannot start with a number.

o Class names typically start with an uppercase letter.

o If the class name includes more than one word, the first letter of each word is usually uppercase, and the rest of the letters are lowercase.

- Classes can have one or more constructors.

o The class constructor is named the same as the class and must be declared as public. Constructors will be explained more in later lessons.

o A constructor is called by using new, followed by the name of the constructor and parentheses. For example, new HelloWord() in the main() method calls the HelloWorld constructor.

- Blocks of code are enclosed in curly brackets, { }, and each line of code ends with a semicolon;

o Every Java program runs the main() method first.

o The main() method calls the class constructor in all the programs in this book. Therefore, the main() method will run first, followed by the class constructor.

o Each statement within the curly brackets is run,

one at a time, in the order it appears in the code.

o Blank lines between lines of code have no effect on how the code runs. Blank lines are added to make the code easier for you to read.

- Print () statements print the text in the parentheses to a window.

o Each print() statement prints on a new line.

o To print a blank line, use print() with empty parentheses.

o The print() method is part of DIYWindow, which is in DIYJava.jar. That's why you added the external JAR file, DIYJava.jar, to the project, and why you chose DIYWindow as the superclass for the HelloWorld class.

- Comments are lines that begin with // or a group of lines that begin with /* and end with */.

CHAPTER - 7

OBJECT-ORIENTED PROGRAMMING

You have learned earlier that Java is an object-oriented programming language. As such, it supports the fundamental principles of this programming paradigm.

An object refers to real entities such as bag, car, chair, or pen. Object-oriented programming languages allow programmers to design programs that use objects and classes. They provide and support features that can simplify software development and maintenance. The most important concepts of this programming paradigm are the following:

- Objects

- Classes

- Method

- Instance

- Inheritance

- Abstraction

- Polymorphism

- Message Parsing

- Encapsulation

Objects

In the real world, you will encounter objects such as humans, dogs, cars, and cats. These objects possess state and behavior. For instance, when you think of a cat, its state can consist of its breed, color, or name. Its behavior may consist of running, jumping, or wagging its tail.

A software object resembles a real-world object in terms of these characteristics. Its state is saved in fields, and its behavior is exhibited through methods.

In development, the methods are performed on an object's internal state, and the methods facilitate communication between objects.

Classes

Classes are used to set the definitions for objects. These specifications serve as blueprints for creating objects. While they are not immediately applied when classes are created, the definitions are available in case an object of the class is instantiated. An object or class can have multiple copies or instances within a program.

Following is an example of a class definition for a class named Cat:

```
public class Cat {
    String breed;
    int ageC
    String color;

    void running() {
    }

    void sleeping() {
    }

    void jum ping() {
    }
}
```

A class can have the following types of variable:

Class variables

Class variables are those that are declared inside a class using the static modifier and outside any method.

Local variables

Local variables are those that are defined within the methods, blocks, or constructors. These variables are declared and instantiated inside the method and are destroyed once the method had been carried out.

Instance variables

Instance variables are those that are inside a class but outside of the methods. They are initialized at the same time as the class. They can be accessed from a method, block, or constructor of that specific class.

A class can contain as many methods as necessary to obtain the values it needs. For example, the Cat class has three methods: running(), sleeping(), and jumping().

Constructors

A constructor is a method which is used to initialize an object. A class must contain at least one constructor.

The following are the important rules for constructors:

The name of the constructor should match the name of the class

It should have no explicit return type.

Types of Constructors

- Default or no-arg constructor

- Parameterized constructor

- Default Constructor

A constructor without a parameter is called default constructor.

Here's the syntax: `<class_nam e>(){}`

Parameterized Constructor

A parameterized constructor is a constructor with parameters. It is used to supply values to specific objects.

The following example shows both types of constructors. The first one is a default constructor, and it doesn't have any parameter. The second constructor has one parameter, the name.

```
public class Kitten {
  public Kitten() {
  }

  public Kitten(String name) {
    // This constructor has one parameter, name.
  }
}
```

Creating Objects

Classes provide the template for objects. Objects are basically created from a class. To create new objects, you will use the 'new' keyword.

The following steps are taken to create a new object from a class:

Declaration—This refers to a variable declaration where you will write the name of the variable and its object type.

Instantiation—To create a new object; you will use the 'new' keyword.

Initialization—A call to a constructor follows the 'new' keyword and initializes a new object.

The following examples show the different steps taken to create a new object from class:

```
public class Kitten {
  public Kitten(String name) {
    // This constructor contains a parameter, the name name.
    System.out.println("Passed Name is:" + name);
  }

  public static void main(String [] args) {
    // Following statement would create an object myPuppy
    Puppy myKitten = new Kitten("spotty");
  }
}
```

Here's the output:

Passed Name is: spotty

How to Access Methods and Instance Variables

The created objects are used to access methods and instance variables. To access instance variables, you will use these steps:

First, you must create an object:

ObjectName = New Constructor();

Next, call a variable like:

ObjectName.variableName;

To call a class method:

ObjectName.MethodName();

Java Package

A package is simply a way of grouping interfaces and classes. A Java package serves as container for classes. The usual basis for grouping is functionality. The use of packages facilitates code reusability. When interfaces and classes are categorized into packages, you can easily access them for use in other programs. The use of packages also helps prevent name conflicts among classes and interfaces.

To create a package, use the package statement before the package name as the first statement.

Here's an example:

```
package m ypack:
public class students
{
...statem ent:
}
```

Import Statement

You may use the import keyword to import packages to your source file. An import statement makes it easy for the compiler to find the location of a class or source code.

You may want to import just one class from a package. You can use the dot operator to indicate the package and the class. For example:

```
im port java.utilDate:
class M yDate extends Date
{
//statem ent.
}
```

To import all classes from one package, you can use the wild character * after the dot operator. For example: `import java.io.*;`

Modifiers

Modifiers are keywords that alter the meaning of the definitions in your code. Java provides several modifiers.

Access Modifiers

The access modifiers are used to define access levels for methods, variables, classes, and constructors.

Private—only accessible within the class

When a method, variable, class, or constructor is declared private, it means that it is only available within the class. If the class, however, has public getter methods, you may be able to access a private variable outside the class. The private keyword indicates the highest access restriction. Take note that you cannot declare interfaces and class as private.

Public—accessible to the world

A method, interface, constructor, class, etc. that has been defined as public may be accessed from other classes. Similarly, blocks, methods, or fields that have been defined inside a public class may be accessed from Java class. This is true as long as they are in the same package. If you want to access a public class from another package, you will have to import the public class. Under the class inheritance concept, subclasses inherit all public variables and methods of a class.

Take note that an application's main() method will have to be declared public before the Java interpreter can call it to run the class.

Protected—accessible to all subclasses and package

Declaring a method, variable, or constructor as protected in a superclass makes it accessible only to classes within its package or to its subclasses in another package. This access type is used if you want to allow the subclass to use variable or helper methods and prevent non-related classes from using them. Interfaces, as well as the fields and methods under them, should not be declared protected, but fields and methods outside of the interface can be declared protected. Classes should not be declared as protected.

Default: Applicable when no modifier is provided—accessible to the package

A method or variable that has been declared without a modifier is accessible to other classes within the package.

The following table summarizes the different access modifiers and their effect:

Modifier	Inside class	Inside package	Outside package by subclass	Outside package
Private	Y	N	N	N
Public	Y	Y	Y	Y
Protected	Y	Y	Y	N
Default	Y	Y	N	N

Non-access Modifiers

The non-access modifiers can be used to access various functionalities in Java.

Final—used to finalize implementations of variables, methods, and classes

Final variables

You can only explicitly initialize a final variable once. When you declare a variable as final, you will never be able to reassign it to another object. Take note, however, that you can still change the data stored inside the object. This means that while you may change the object's state, you will not be able to change the reference. The final modifier is commonly paired with static to create a class variable out of the constant value.

Final methods

The final keyword is used to prevent a method from being changed by subclasses.

Final classes

The final modifier is used to prevent other classes from inheriting any feature from the class declared as a final class.

Static—used to create class methods or variables.

You can use this keyword to create a unique variable (called a static variable or class variable) that will exist independently from other instances of the class. You cannot declare a local variable as static.

You can also use the static keyword to create a method (called a static method or class method) that will exist independently from other instances of the class. Static methods recognize and work only on data from the arguments given without considering variables.

You may access class methods and class variables by writing the variable or method name after the class name and a dot (.).

Abstract—used to create abstract methods or classes

Abstract class

When a class is declared as abstract, it means that you will never be able to instantiate the class. The only reason for declaring a class as abstract is to extend the class. You cannot declare a class to be both final and abstract, as you can't possibly extend a final class. A class that uses abstract methods will have to be declared as abstract. Failure to do so will result in compile errors.

Abstract method

As it is declared with no implementation, an abstract method derives its methods body from the subclass. Abstract methods cannot be declared as strict or final. Unless it is also an abstract class, a class extending an abstract class must adopt the abstract methods of the superclass. A class that contains at least one abstract method should be declared as an abstract class. On the other hand, an abstract class need not have abstract methods.

Example:

```
abstract class Car {
    private double price;
    private String type;
    private String year;
    public abstract void goFast();   // abstract method
    public abstract void changeColor();
```

Synchronized

The synchronized modifier is used to indicate that only one thread can access a method at any given time. You can use this keyword with any access level modifier.

Example:

```
public synchronized void showInfo() {
    ........
}
```

Volatile

This keyword is used to indicate that a thread accessing a volatile variable should merge its private copy with the master copy stored in memory. In effect, it synchronizes all cached copies of the variable with the main memory. You may only use this modifier to define instance variables of the private or object type.

Example:

```
public class MyRunnable implements Runnable {
    private volatile boolean active:

    public void run() {
        active = true:
        while (active) {   // line 1
            // code here
        }
    }

    public void stop() {
        active = false:   // line 2
    }
}
```

Transient

The keyword transient is used to tell the compiler to skip an instance variable when it is serializing the object that contains the marked variable.

Example:

```
public transient int limit = 50:   // will not persist
```

CHAPTER - 8

DECISION MAKING AND LOOP CONTROL

The decision making structures are used in situations where a set of instructions have to be executed if the condition is true and another set of instructions have to be executed when the condition is determined to be false. There are several constructs available in Java for programming such scenarios. These structures include—

If statement

This statement is used in situations where a condition needs to be tested, and if the condition is found true, the block of code that follows this statement needs to be executed.

The syntax for this construct is—

```
if(condition){
/*Body*/
}
```

Sample implementation for this construct is given below—

```
public class ifDemo {
public static void main(String args[]) {
int i = 10;
int j = 1;
if(i>j){
System.out.print(i);
}
}
}
```

If else statement

This statement is used in situations where a condition needs to be tested, and if the condition is found true, the block of code that follows this statement needs to be executed else the block of code that follows the else statement is executed. The syntax for this construct is—

```
if(condition){

/*Body*/

}

else(

/*Body*/

}
```

Sample implementation for this construct is given below—

```java
public class ifElseDemo {
public static void main(String args[]) {
int i = 1;
int j = 0;
if(i>j){
System.out.print(i);
}
else{
System.out.print(j);
}
}
}
```

Nested if statement

This statement is used in situations where a condition needs to be tested, and if the condition is found true, the block of code that follows this statement needs to be executed else the next condition is tested. If this condition is found true, the block of code corresponding to the if statement for this condition is executed. If none of the conditions are found true, the block of code that follows the else statement is executed. Multiple conditions can be tested using the nested if statements. The syntax for this construct is—

```
if(condition1) {

/*Body*/

}

else if (condition2) (

/*Body*/

}

else {

/*Body*/

}
```

Sample implementation for this construct is given below—

```java
public class nestedIfDemo {
public static void main(String args[]) {
int i = 0;
int j = 0;
if(i>j){
System.out.print(i);
}
else if(j>i) {
System.out.print(j);
}
else {
System.out.print("Equal");
}
}
}
```

Switch

If you have a variable and different blocks of code need to be executed for different values of that variable, the ideal construct that can be used is the switch statement. The syntax for this construct is—

```
switch(variable){

case <value1>:

/*body*/

break;

case <value2>:

/*body*/

break;

case <value3>:
```

```
/*body*/

break;

default:

/*body*/

break;

}
```

Sample implementation for this construct is given below—

```java
public class switchDemo {
public static void main(String args[]) {
int i = 5;
switch (i) {
case 0:
System.out.print(0);
break;
case 2:
System.out.print(2);
break;
```

```java
case 5:
System.out.print(5);
break;
default:
System.out.print(999);
break;
}
}
}
```

Conditional Operator

Java also supports the conditional operator, which is also known as the?: operator. This operator is used to replace the 'if else' construct. Its syntax is as follows—

Expression1? Expression2: Expression3

Here, Expression1 is the condition that is to be tested. If the condition is true, Expression2 is executed else Expression3 is executed.

Loop Control

There are several situations that require you to iterate the same set of instructions a number of times. For instance, if you need to sort a set of numbers, you will need to scan and rearrange the set several times to get the desired arrangement. This flow of execution is known as loop control.

Simply, a loop is a construct that allows the execution of a block of code many times. Java supports several constructs that can be used for implementing loops. These include a while loop, for loop, and do while loop.

A while loop executes a block of code iteratively until the condition specified for the while loop is true. The moment this condition fails, while loop stops.

For loop allows the programmer to manipulate the condition and loop variable in the same construct.

Therefore, you can initialize a loop variable, increment/decrement it, and run the loop until a condition on this variable is true.

Do while loop is similar to while loop. However, in the while loop, the condition is checked before executing the block code. On the other hand, in a do while loop, the block of code is executed, and then the condition is checked. If the condition is satisfied, the loop execution is again initiated else the loop is terminated. It would not be wrong to state that the do while loop, once implemented, will execute at least once.

Loop statements

There are two keywords that are specifically used in connection with loops and are also termed as control statements as they allow transfer of control from one section of the code to a different section. These keywords are—

Break

This keyword is used inside the loop at a point where you want the execution flow to terminate the loop and directly start execution from the first instruction that appears after the loop.

Continue

This keyword is used inside the loop at a point where the programmer wants the computer to overlook the rest of the loop and move the control to the first statement of the loop.

In order to help you understand how loops are executed, let us take an example and implement it using all the three types of loop control.

For Loop Implementation

```
public class forDemo {

public static void main(String args[]) {

int [] numberArray = {100, 300, 500, 700, 900};

for(int i=0; i<5; i++) {

System.out.print(numberArray[i]);

System.out.print(,"");

}

System.out.print("\n");

}

}
```

While Loop Implementation

```
public class whileDemo {
public static void main(String args[]) {
int [] numberArray = {100, 300, 500, 700, 900};
int i = 0;
while(i<5) {
System.out.print(numberArray[i]);
System.out.print(",");
i++;
}
System.out.print("\n");
}
}
```

Do While Loop Implementation

```java
public class doWhileDemo {
public static void main(String args[]) {
int [] numberArray = {100, 300, 500, 700, 900};
int i = 0;
do {
System.out.print(numberArray[i]);
System.out.print(",");
i++;
} while (i<5);
System.out.print("\n");
}
}
```

Enhanced For Loop

Java also supports an enhanced loop structure, which can be used for array elements. The syntax for this loop construct is—

```
for(declaration : expression) {

/*Body*/

}
```

The declaration part of the Enhanced for loop is used to declare a variable. This variable shall be local to the 'for loop' and must have the same type as the type of the array elements. The current value of the variable is always equal to the array element that is being traversed in the loop. The expression is an array or a method call that returns an array.

Sample implementation of the enhanced for loop has been given below -

```java
public class forArrayDemo {
public static void main(String args[]) {
int [] numberArray = {100, 300, 500, 700, 900};
for(int i : numberArray ) {
System.out.print( i );
System.out.print(",");
}
System.out.print("\n");
}
}
```

Exception Hierarchy

Java has an inbuilt class named java.lang.Exception and all the exceptions fall under this class. All the exception classes are subclasses of this class. Moreover, the Throwable class is the superclass of the exception class. Another subclass of the Throwable class is the Error class. All the errors like stack overflow described above fall under this Error class.

The Exception class has two subclasses, namely RuntimeException class and IOException class. A list of the methods, for which definitions are available in Java, as part of the Throwable class, is given below.

```
public String getMessage()
```

When called, this message returns a detailed description of the exception that has been encountered.

```
public Throwable getCause()
```

This method, when called returns a message that contains the cause of the exception.

```
public String toString()
```

This method returns the detailed description of the exception concatenated with the name of the class.

```
public void printStackTrace()
```

The result of toString(), along with a trace of the stack, can be printed to the standard error stream, System.err, can be done by calling this method.

```
public StackTraceElement [] getStackTrace()
```

There may be some scenarios where you may need to access different elements of the stack trace. This method returns an array, with each element of the stack trace saved to different elements of the array. The first element of the array contains the top element of the stack trace, while the bottom of the stack trace is saved to the last element of the array.

```
public Throwable fillInStackTrace()
```

Appends the previous information in the stack trace with the current contents of the stack trace and returns the same as an array.

Catching Exceptions

The standard method to catch an exception is using the 'try and catch' keywords along with their code implementations. This try and catch block needs to be implemented in such a manner that it encloses the code that is expected to raise an exception. It is also important to mention here that the code that is expected to raise an exception is termed as protected code. The syntax for try and catch block implementation is as follows—

```
try {

/*Protected code*/

}catch(ExceptionName exc1) {

/*Catch code*/

}
```

The code that is expected to raise an exception is placed inside the try block. If the exception is raised, then the corresponding action to be performed for exception handling is implemented in the catch block. It is imperative for every try block to either have a catch block or a final block.

As part of the catch statement, the exception, which is expected to be raised needs to be declared. In the event that an exception occurs, the execution is transferred to the catch block. If the raised exception matches the exception defined in the catch block, the catch block is executed.

A sample implementation of the try and catch block is given below. The code implements an array with 2 elements. However, the code tries to access the third element, which does not exist. As a result, an exception is raised.

```
try {

/*Protected code*/

}catch(ExceptionName exc1) {

/*Catch code*/

}

int arr[] = new int[2];

System.out.println("Accesing the 3rd element of the array:" + arr[3]);

}catch(ArrayIndexOutOfBoundsException exp) {
```

```
System.out.println("Catching Exception:" + exp);

}

System.out.println("Reached    outside    catch
block");

}

}
```

Implementing Multiple Catch Blocks

A block of code may lead to multiple exceptions. In order to cater for this requirement, implementation of multiple catch blocks is also allowed. The syntax for such implementation is given below.

```
try {

/*Protected Code*/

}catch(ExpType1 exp1) {

/*Catch block 1*/

}catch(ExpType2 exp2) {

/*Catch block 2*/

}catch(ExpType3 exp3) {

/*Catch block 3*/

}
```

The syntax shown above has illustrated the implementation of three catch blocks. However, you can implement as many catch blocks as you want. When this code is executed, the protected is executed. If an exception occurs, the type of exception is matched with the exception of the first catch block. However, if the exception type does not match, the catch block 1 is ignored, and the exception type for the second catch block is tried for matching. Whichever catch block has the same exception type as that of the raised exception; the corresponding catch block is executed.

CHAPTER - 9

ADT, DATA STRUCTURE, AND JAVA COLLECTIONS

An abstract data type (ADT) is a logical description of the data and the operations that are allowed on it. ADT is defined as a user point of view of a data. ADT concerns about the possible values of the data and the interface exposed by it. ADT does not concern about the actual implementation of the data structure.

For example, a user wants to store some integers and find their mean value. ADT for this data structure will support two functions, one for adding integers and other to get mean value. ADT for this data structure does not talk about how exactly it will be implemented.

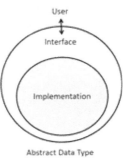

Abstract Data Type

Data-Structure

Data structures are concrete representations of data and are defined as a programmer point of view of data. Data-structure represents how data will be stored in memory. All data-structures have their own pros and cons. Depending upon the type of problem, we choose a data-structure that is best suited for it.

For example, we can store data in an array, a linked-list, stack, queue, tree, etc.

Note: In this chapter, we will be studying various data structures and their API. So that the user can use them without knowing their internal implementation.

JAVA Collection Framework

JAVA programming language provides a JAVA Collection Framework, which is a set of high quality, high performance & reusable data-structures and algorithms.

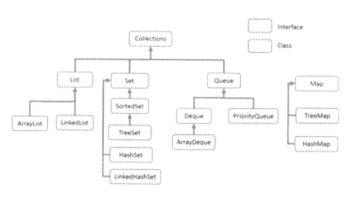

The following advantages of using a JAVA collection framework:

1. Programmers do not have to implement basic data structures and algorithms repeatedly. Thereby it prevents the reinvention of the wheel. Thus, the programmer can devote more effort in business logic

2. The JAVA Collection Framework code is well-tested, high quality, high-performance code. Using them increase the quality of the programs.

3. Development cost is reduced as basic data structures and algorithms are implemented in the Collections framework are reused.

4. Easy to review and understand programs written by other developers as most of Java developers uses the Collection framework. In addition, the collection framework is well documented.

Array

Array represents a collection of multiple elements of the same datatypes.

Array ADT Operations

Below is the API of the array:

1. Adds an element at the kth position. Value can be stored in an array at Kth position in O(1) constant time. We just need to store value at arr[k].

2. Reading the value stored at the kth position.

Accessing the value stored at some index in the array is also O(1) constant time. We just need to read the value stored at arr[k].

3. Substitution of value stored in the kth position with a new value. Time complexity: O(1) constant time.

Example:

```java
public class ArrayDemo {
    public static void main(String[] args) {
        int[] arr = new int[10];
        for (int i = 0; i < 10; i++)
        {
            arr[i] = i;
        }
    }
}
```

JAVA standard arrays are of fixed length. Sometimes we do not know how much memory we need, so we create a bigger size array. Thereby wasting space. If an array is already full and we want to add more values to it than we need to create a new array, which has sufficient space and then copy the old array to the new array. To avoid this manual reallocation and copy, we can use ArrayList of JAVA Collection framework or Linked Lists to store data.

ArrayList implementation in JAVA Collections

ArrayList<E> in JAVA Collections is a data structure which implements List<E> interface, which means that it can have duplicate elements in it. ArrayList is an implementation as a dynamic array that can grow or shrink as needed. (Internally array is used when it is full a bigger array is allocated, and the old array values are copied to it).

Example:

```java
import java.util.ArrayList;
public class ArrayListDemo {
    public static void main(String[] args) {
        ArrayList<Integer> al = new ArrayList<Integer>();
        al.add(1); // add 1 to the end of the list
        al.add(2); // add 2 to the end of the list
        System.out.println("Contents of Array: " + al);
        System.out.println("Array Size: " + al.size());
        System.out.println("Array IsEmpty: " +
```

```java
public static void main(String[] args) {
    ArrayList<Integer> al = new ArrayList<Integer>();
    al.add(1); // add 1 to the end of the list
    al.add(2); // add 2 to the end of the list
    System.out.println("Contents of Array: " + al);
    System.out.println("Array Size: " + al.size());
    System.out.println("Array IsEmpty: " + al.isEmpty());
    al.remove(al.size() -1); // last element of array is removed.
    al.removeAll(al); // all the elements of array are removed.
    System.out.println("Array IsEmpty: " + al.isEmpty());
}
}
```

Output:

Linked List

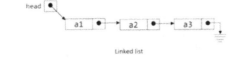

Linked list

Linked lists are a dynamic data structure, and memory is allocated at run time. The concept of the linked list is not to store data contiguously. Nodes of the linked list contain a link that points to the next elements in the list.

Performance-wise linked lists are slower than arrays because there is no direct access to linked list elements. Linked list is a useful data structure when we do not know the number of elements to be stored ahead of time. There are many types of linked lists: linear, circular, doubly, doubly circulare, etc.

Linked list ADT Operations

Below is the API of Linked list.

Insert(k): adds k to the start of the list

Insert an element at the start of the list. Just create a new element and move pointers. So that this new element becomes the first element of the list. This operation will take O(1) constant time.

Delete(): Delete the element at the start of the list

Delete an element at the start of the list. We just need to move one pointer. This operation will also take O(1) constant time.

PrintList(): Display all the elements of the list.

Start with the first element and then follow the pointers. This operation will take O(N) time.

Find(k): Find the position of the element with value k

Start with the first element and follow the pointer until we get the value we are looking for or reach the end of the list. This operation will take O(N) time.

Note: Binary search does not work on linked lists.

FindKth(k): Find element at position k

Start from the first element and follow the links until you reach the kth element. This operation will take O(N) time.

IsEmpty(): Check if the number of elements in the list are zero.

Just check the head pointer of the list, if it is Null,

then the list is empty otherwise not empty. This operation will take O(1) time.

LinkedList implementation in JAVA Collections

LinkedList<E> in by JAVA Collections is a data structure that also implements List<E> interface.

Example:

```
import java.util.LinkedList;

public class LinkedListDemo {

    public static void main(String[] args) {

        LinkedList<Integer> ll = new LinkedList<Integer>();

        ll.addFirst(2); // 8 is added to the list

        ll.addLast(10); // 9 is added to last of the list.

        ll.addFirst(1); // 7 is added to first of the list.

        ll.addLast(11); // 20 is added to last of the list

        System.out.println("Contents of Linked List: " + ll);

        ll.removeFirst();

        ll.removeLast();
```

```
            System.out.println("Contents of Linked
List: " + ll);

        }

}
```

Output:

```
Contents of Linked List: [1, 2, 10, 11]

Contents of Linked List: [2, 10]
```

Stack

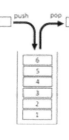

Stack is a special kind of data structure that follows the Last-In-First-Out (LIFO) strategy. This means that the element that is added last will be the first to be removed.

The various applications of the stack are:

Recursion: recursive calls are implemented using system stack.

1. Postfix evaluation of the expression.

2. Backtracking implemented using stack.

3. Depth-first search of trees and graphs.

4. Converting a decimal number into a binary number etc.

Stack ADT Operations

Push(k): Adds value k to the top of the stack

Pop(): Remove element from the top of the stack and return its value.

Top(): Returns the value of the element at the top of the stack

Size(): Returns the number of elements in the stack

IsEmpty(): determines whether the stack is empty. It returns true if the stack is empty otherwise return false.

Note: All the above stack operations are implemented in O(1) Time Complexity.

Stack implementation in JAVA Collection

The stack is implemented by calling push and pop methods of Stack <T> class.

Example:

```
public class StackDemo {

    public static void main(String[] args) {

        Stack<Integer> stack = new Stack<Integer>();
```

```java
        int temp;
        stack.push(1);
        stack.push(2);
        stack.push(3);
        System.out.println("Stack : "+stack);
        System.out.println("Stack size : "+stack.
size());
        System.out.println("Stack pop : "+stack.
pop());
        System.out.println("Stack top : "+stack.
peek());
        System.out.println("Stack isEmpty : 
"+stack.isEmpty());
    }
}
```

Output:

```
Stack : [1, 2, 3]
Stack size : 3
Stack pop : 3
```

```
Stack : [1, 2, 3]

Stack size : 3

Stack pop : 3

Stack top : 2

Stack isEmpty : false
```

Stack is also implemented by calling push and pop methods of ArrayDeque<T> class.

JDK provides both ArrayDeque<T> and Stack<T>. We can use both of these classes. But there are some advantages of ArrayDeque<T>.

1. First reason is that Stack<T> does not drive from Collection interface.

2. Second Stack<T> drives from Vector<T> so random access is possible, so it brakes abstraction of a stack.

3. Third ArrayDeque is more efficient as compared to Stack<T>.

Queue

A queue is a First-In-First-Out (FIFO) kind of data structure. The element that is added to the queue first will be the first to be removed, and so on.

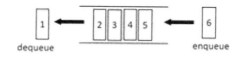

dequeue   enqueue

Queue has the following application uses:

1. Access to shared resources (e.g., printer)

2. Multiprogramming

3. Message queue

4. BFS, breadth-first traversal of graph or tree are implemented using queue.

Queue ADT Operations:

Add(K): Adds a new element k to the back of the queue.

Remove(): Removes an element from the front of the queue and return its value.

Front(): Returns the value of the element at the front of the queue.

Size(): Returns the number of elements inside the queue.

IsEmpty(): Returns 1 if the queue is empty otherwise returns 0

Note: All the above queue operations are implemented in O(1) Time Complexity.

Queue implementation in JAVA Collection

ArrayDeque<T> is the class implementation of a

doubly ended queue. If we use add(), remove() and peek () it will behave like a queue. (Moreover, if we use push(), pop(), and peekLast() it behave like a stack.)

Example:

```java
import java.util.ArrayDeque;
public class QueueDemo {
    public static void main(String[] args) {
        ArrayDeque<Integer> que = new ArrayDeque<Integer>();
        que.add(1);
        que.add(2);
        que.add(3);
        System.out.println("Queue : "+que);
        System.out.println("Queue size : "+que.size());
        System.out.println("Queue peek : "+que.peek());
    }
```

Output:

```
Queue size : 3

Queue peek : 1

Queue remove : 1

Queue isEmpty : false
```

CHAPTER - 10

FILE HANDLING

This chapter discusses the details of reading, writing, creating, and opening files. There are a wide array of file I/O classes and methods to choose from.

Reading a text File

Reading a text file is a crucial ability in Java and has many practical applications. FileReader, BufferedReader, and Scanner are useful classes for reading a plain text file in Java. Each of them possess specific qualities that make them uniquely qualified to handle certain situations.

BufferedReader

This technique reads text from a stream of character input. It buffers characters, arrays, and rows to be read efficiently. You can specify the buffer type or use the standard type. For most reasons, the default is big enough. In particular, each read application produced from a Reader leads the fundamental personality or byte stream to make a respective read application. Therefore, it is advisable to wrap a BufferedReader around any Reader whose read) (transactions, like FileReaders and InputStreamReaders, can be expensive.

For example:

```
BufferedReaderin=NewBufferedReader(Reader in, int size)
```

FileReader

Class of convenience to read character documents. This class ' constructors suppose the default character format and the default byte-buffer size is suitable.

Scanner

A simple text scanner that uses regular expressions to parse primitive types and strings. A Scanner uses a delimiter model to break its entry into tokens that suits white space by definition. Using distinct next techniques, the resulting tokens can then be transformed into values of distinct kinds.

```
import java.io.File;

import java.util.Scanner;
```

```java
public class ReadFromFileUsingScanner

{

public static void main(String[] args) throws
Exception

{

// filepath is set as a parameter now so that it
can be scanned
```

File example =

```java
new          File("C:\\Users\\userName\\Desktop\\
example.txt");

Scanner example1 = new Scanner(file);

while (example1.hasNextLine())

System.out.println(example1.nextLine());

}

}
```

Using Scanner class but without using loops:

```java
import java.io.File;

import java.io.FileNotFoundException;
```

```java
import java.util.Scanner;

public class example{

public static void main(String[] args)

throws FileNotFoundException {

File example = new File("C:\\Users\\userName\\Desktop\\example.txt");

Scanner example1 = new Scanner(file);

// we will use \\Z as a delimiter

sc.useDelimiter("\\Z");

System.out.println(example1.next());

}

}
```

Read a text file as String in Java

```java
package io;

import java.nio.file.*;;

public class example{

public static example(String fileName)throws Exception {

String example1 = "";
```

```java
example1 = new String(Files.readAllBytes(Paths.get(fileName)));

return example1;

}

public static void main(String[] args) throws Exception

{

String example1 = example("C:\\Users\\userName\\Desktop\\example.java");

System.out.println(example1);

}

}
```

Writing to a text file

You can use one of the write methods to write bytes or lines to a file. Write methods include:

- Write(Path, byte[], OpenOption...)

- Write(Path, Iterable< extends CharSequence>, Charset, OpenOption...)

Renaming and Deleting Files

Renaming

In Java, there's a method called renameTo(fileName) within the File class that we can use to rename a file.

Deleting Files

Files that are saved using the java program will be permanently removed without moving to the trash/recycle bin. Using java.io.File.delete deletes this abstract pathname from the file or folder. Using java.nio.file.files.deleteifexists will delete a folder, if it occurs. If the folder is not open, it also deletes a folder listed in the route.

Advanced Topics In Java

Generics

In any non-trivial software project, bugs are simply a fact of life. Careful planning, programming, and testing may help diminish their omnipresence, but somehow they will always find a way to enter your system somewhere. This becomes especially apparent as new features are introduced, and your code base's magnitude and complexity increases.

Fortunately, it is easier to detect some bugs than others. Compile-time bugs, for instance, can be identified soon; you can use the compiler's error codes to determine what the issue is and solve it, right then and there. Runtime bugs, however, can be much harder; they do not always occur instantly, and when they do, they may be at a point in the program far apart from the true cause of the problem. Generics help stabilize your software by creating it feasible at compile time to identify more of your bugs.

Generics, in a nutshell, allow parameters for kinds (classes and objects) when defining courses, interfaces, and techniques. Like the more familiar formal parameters used in declarations of methods, type parameters provide you with distinct outputs to re-use the same code. The distinction is that values are the inputs to formal parameters, while kinds are the answers to type parameters. Code using generics has many advantages over the non-generic code. Through the use of generics, programmers can introduce generic algorithms that operate on distinct kinds of collections, can be tailored, and are secure and simpler to read form.

Generic Types

A generic form is a types-parameterized generic category or interface. It is possible to modify an easy box class to show the idea. Consider a non-generic box category that works on any sort of object. It only requires to provide two techniques: set), (adding an item to the cabinet, and get), (retrieving it. Because their methods accept or return an object, you are free to pass in whatever you want, as long as it is not one of the primitive types. There is no way to check how the class is used at compile time. One portion of the software may put an integer in the cabinet and expect to get integers out of it, while another portion of the software may erroneously move through a string, leading in a mistake in runtime.

The segment of the type parameter, delegated by angle brackets (< >), displays the title of the category. It indicates the parameters of the form (also known as factors of the sort) T1, T2, till T. You generate a generic type statement by altering the file "government class box" to "government class box <T >" to update the box category to use generics. This presents the type variable, T, which can be used inside the class anywhere. This replaces all Object events with T. Any non-primitive type you specify can be a type variable: any type of class, any type of interface, any type of array, or even some other type variable. It is possible to apply this same method to generic interfaces.

Type designations are single, upper case letters by convention. This contrasts sharply with the variable naming conventions you already understand about and with an excellent reason: it would be hard to say the distinction between a type variable and a normal class or object name without this convention.

The most commonly used type parameter names are:

- E - Element (used extensively by the Java Collections Framework)
- K - Key
- N - Number
- T - Type
- V - Value
- S,U,V, etc.—2nd, 3rd, 4th types

You'll see these names used throughout the JDK and the API.

Invoking and Instantiating a Generic Type

To mention the generic box category within your system, a generic type invocation must be performed that brings T with a certain concrete value, such as Integer:

```
Box<Integer> integerBox;
```

You may believe that an invocation of a generic sort is comparable to a normal process invocation, but instead of adding an assertion to a procedure, you transfer a type argument—Integer, in this case—to the box category itself.

Many designers interchangeably use the words "type parameter" and "type statement," but not the same definitions. When coding, to generate a parameterized type, one offers sort arguments. The T in Foo < T > is, therefore, a type parameter, and the Foo < String > f string is a type contention. In using these words, this class follows this concept.

Like any other statement of variable, this software does not generate a fresh item of the box. It merely states that integerBox will have a reference to an "Integer Box," which is how it reads Box < Integer>. A generic type invocation is usually referred to as a parameterized type.

To instantiate this class, use the new keyword, as usual, but place <Integer> between the class name and the parenthesis:

```
Box<Integer> integerBox = new Box<Integer>();
```

The Diamond

In the latest versions of Java, you can replace the type arguments needed to invoke a generic class constructor with an empty set of type arguments (< >) as long as the compiler can determine, or infer from the context, the type arguments. This angle bracket couple, < >, is called "The Diamond loosely." For example, you can use the previous declaration to generate an instance of Box < Integer>:

```
Box<Integer> integerBox = new Box<>();
```

Generic Methods

Generic techniques are techniques which implement parameters of their own sort. This is similar to a generic type declaration, but the scope of the type parameter is limited to the method in which it is declared. In addition to generic class constructors, static and non-static generic techniques are permitted.

The syntax for a generic technique involves a list of parameters of type inside angle brackets that appear before the return type of the procedure. The type parameter segment must occur before the return type of the method for static generic techniques. The Util class involves, compare, a generic technique comparing two Pair items.

```
Pair<Integer, String> ex1 = new Pair<>(49,
"string1");

Pair<Integer, String> ex2 = new Pair<>(64,
"string2");

boolean     comparison     =     Util.<Integer,
String>compare(ex1, ex2);
```

Bounded Type Parameters

Sometimes you want to limit the kinds that can be used in a parameterized type as form statements. For instance, a technique that works on figures could only recognize Number cases or its subclasses. That's what limit parameters of the sort are for.

List the name of the type parameter to indicate a defined type parameter, accompanied by the extension's keyword, followed by the upper bound, which is Number in this instance. Note that expands is generally used in this context to mean either "extends" (as in courses) or "implements" (as in interfaces).

Multiple Bounds

Type parameters can have more than one bound. A type variable with multiple bounds is a subtype of all the types listed in the bound. If one of the bounds is a class, it must be specified first. For example:

```
Class X { /* ... */ }

interface Y { /* ... */ }

interface Z { /* ... */ }

class R <T extends X & Y & Z> { /* ... */ }
```

If bound X is not specified first, you get a compile-time error:

```
class R <T extends Y & X & Z> { /* ... */ } // compile-time error
```

CHAPTER - 11

COLLECTIONS

Functionalizing Collections

When we externalize code, we expose every step. This is the hallmark of imperative programming. However, one of the re-occurring themes of functional programming is the idea of doing the exact opposite: internalizing code. The act of internalizing code is to hide the details inside a function. But functional programming pushes this idea further by turning micro-patterns of everyday programming into functions. For example, iterating over data, be it with iterators, for-loops, or while-loops, is one of those micro-patterns. Functional programming changes the way we think about them.

Java's functionalization effort would not be complete without a revamp of its Collections library, namely the Collection, Map, List, and Set interfaces. This is because iteration is often done over collections, and they are the very fabric of Java programs. It is a natural place for the functionalization effort to occur. But making any kind of significant changes, like adding new methods to the Collection interface, would break backward compatibility to all programs written pre-Java 8. This includes not only the JDK's own hierarchy extending the Collection interface but any open or closed source 3rd party library and in-house classes. Java's designers never have and will never adopt such a strategy. Yet changes were necessary; the library was introduced in 1998, eons in software industry years, and was showing its age.

The motivation for the introduction of default methods was ushered by the need to modernize and functionalize the Collections library. Default methods are just the right tonic because they permit behavior to be added at the root of the hierarchy without disturbing dependent classes. Subclasses can either inherit or override the behavior. Unlike adding new interface methods, subclasses can automatically accept new default methods without recompilation. Instant compatibility is achieved. Default methods have proven useful in their own right but owe their existence to the need to functionalize the Collections library.

A second re-occurring theme in functional programming is parallelization. Quite simply, functional programming offers a better mousetrap for parallel processing. As a consequence, the

Collections library has been enriched to benefit from multi-core CPUs when processing collections. Together with Streams, the Collections library is at center stage in bringing functional-style parallel processing to Java.

Now that we've studied Java's standard functional interfaces, we can begin to apply that knowledge to Collections. Let's look at what has become of the Collections library in Java 8.

Collection interface

We start by looking at a brand new default method in the Collection interface available to lists and sets. This is the forEach() method:

```
// Defined in the Iterable interface and extended in Collection
default void forEach (Consumer<? super T> action)
```

This method iterates through the entire collection letting the Consumer decide what to do for each element. This is the concept of internal iteration and a manifestation of declarative programming. The details of how to iterate are not specified. This is in opposition to external iteration, where the details of how to iterate as well as what to do with each element are specified in code.

We will show examples of these functionalized collection methods with the slapstick comedy trio from the golden age of Hollywood films: Larry, Moe, and Curly of The Three Stooges fame. To start, let's print the contents of a collection:

```
Collection<String> stooges = Arrays.asList("Larry", "Moe", "Curly");
// Print the contents of the stooges collection
stooges.forEach(System.out::println);
```

The forEach() method has a very wide range of applicability. It is a much more convenient way to iterate through collections and should be your de-facto standard. However, being a declarative construct, there are some things you will not be able to do. Most notably, you cannot change the state of local variables like you could in a while-loop. Algorithms must be re-thought functionally. For now, just know that forEach() is ideal for iterations that do not mutate state.

We now look at another new method available in Collection:

```
default boolean removeIf(Predicate<? super E> filter)
```

The method removeIf() internalizes the entire process of iterating, testing, and removing. It requires only to be told what the condition for removal is.

Using the now-familiar predicate functional interface, we can easily figure out what kind of lambda to use.

```
// Remove all people not part of The Three Stooges comedy trio
List<String> theThreeStooges = new ArrayList<>
    (Arrays.asList("Larry", "Moe", "Curly", "Tom", "Dick", "Harry"));

// Create the predicate that determines who is a stooge
Predicate<String> isAStooge =
    s -> "Larry".equals(s) || "Moe".equals(s) || "Curly".equals(s);

// Negate the condition to remove non-stooges
theThreeStooges.removeIf (isAStooge.negate());
```

To replace all contents of a List, we can use replaceAll():

```
List<String> theThreeStooges = new ArrayList<>
    (Arrays.asList("Larry", "Moe", "Curly"));

// Create the lambda to feminize the names
UnaryOperator<String> feminize =
    s -> "Larry".equals(s) ? "Lara" : "Moe".equals(s) ? "Maude" : "Shirley";

// Replace all male names with their female counterparts
theThreeStooges.replaceAll (feminize);
```

ReplaceAll() uses a UnaryOperator as its functional interface, which is a Function sub interface.

Both replaceIf() and replaceAll() are available to all subclasses with one caveat: the underlying class must support removal, or an exception will be thrown.

These examples show the compactness of functional programming. Most of the work was done by the function with the lambda providing the details.

Map interface

One of the biggest irritants of using lists as values in maps is the constant need to check for the presence of the map before adding, updating, or removing an element. First, you must try to extract the list and create it if it is not found. For example, say we have a method that updates a movie database implemented as a Map. The map's key is the year of the movie, and its value is a list of movies for that year. Pre-Java 8, the code would look like this:

```
private Map<Integer, List<String>> movieDatabase = new HashMap<>();

private void addMovie(Integer year, String title) {
    List<String> movies = movieDatabase.get(year);

    if (movies == null) {
        // Need to create the array list if it doesn't yet exist
        movies = new LinkedList<String>();
        movieDatabase.put(year, movies);
    }

    movies.add(title);
}
```

Java 8 offers a better alternative with these default methods:

```
default V compute
    (K key,
     BiFunction<? super K, ? super V, ? extends V> remappingFunction)

default V computeIfPresent
    (K key,
     BiFunction<? super K, ? super V, ? extends V> remappingFunction)

default V computeIfAbsent
    (K key,
     Function<? super K, ? extends V> mappingFunction)

default V getOrDefault (Object key, V defaultValue);

default V putIfAbsent (K key, V value);

default V merge
    (K key, V value,
     BiFunction<? super V, ? super V, ? extends V> remappingFunction)
```

Let's start with the compute methods. Each variant allows the map's value to be generated by the mapping function. For computeIfPresent() and computeIfAbsent(), mapping occurs conditionally. So with these methods, we can refactor the previous code example:

```java
private Map<Integer, List<String>> movieDatabase = new HashMap<>();

private void addMovie(Integer year, String title) {
    movieDatabase.computeIfAbsent (year, k -> new LinkedList<>());
    movieDatabase.compute (year,
      (k, v) -> {
          // K is the key of the map (the year)
          // V is the value containing the list strings (titles)
          v.add(title);
          return v;
      });
}
```

Notice that the creation of the list is handled by the computeIfAbsent() lambda. When it is time to add the movie to the list, via the compute() method, the add() will never throw a NullPointerException because the list is guaranteed to have been created.

In this case, using the computeIfAbsent() method is overkill, and we would be better off with putIfAbsent():

```java
movieDatabase.putIfAbsent (year, new LinkedList<>());
```

This method is lambda-less and expects a value to be given—not calculated. This is still a functional style method even though no lambda was used. It proves the point that you can express code functionally without necessarily using lambdas.

If you still need to extract the data, you can use a more functional approach with the getOrDefault() method:

```java
movieDatabase.getOrDefault (year, new LinkedList<>());
```

You can also use the merge() method as an alternative. It facilitates the checking of the existence of a list. In the example below, if the key (year) doesn't exist in the map, it puts the value (titles) on the map. If it does exist, it allows a BiFunction to decide what to do with the two lists:

```
private Map<Integer, List<String>> movieDatabase = new HashMap<>();

private void addMovies(Integer year, List<String> titles) {
    // Merge the contents of the current list at key=year with titles
    movieDatabaseb.merge (year, titles,
        (t1, t2) -> {
            // Append titles to current list - only gets called if
            // a value is stored at this key. Otherwise, titles is
            // stored.
            t1.addAll(t2);
            return t1;
        });
}
```

And it can be used this way:

```
List<String> titles = new ArrayList<>(
    Arrays.asList("Meet the Baron", "Nertsery Rhymes"));

movieDatabaseb.merge (1933, titles,
    // BiFunction to append t2 to t1
    (t1, t2) -> {t1.addAll(t2); return t1;});
```

The BiFunction can also return null, which tells the merge to delete the key.

The takeaway is that we have removed the overhead code of checking for the existence of an element and can now focus on what really matters: defining how to create the list and how to add an element to the list.

The map interface has been enriched with other

functional methods such as forEach(), replace(), and replaceAll() and uses the same principle of code internalization. Consult the appendix for the complete listing.

Spliterator

The Collections library is still subject to the same constraints regarding concurrent access. As always, you must choose the Collections library class that corresponds to your thread safety requirements. This is because the new methods shown above are just functional abstractions riding above the same underlying data structures. These methods are not particularly amenable to functional programming's take on parallel processing because they are still based on the notion of multiple threads mutating the collection and synchronizing access to the underlying data. However, there exists a new Java 8 abstraction that is compatible. It is designed to iterate over data in parallel. The idea is embodied by the Spliterator interface. The premise of this interface is to partition the data and handoff chunks to different threads. Spliterators can be obtained from the Collection interface, including subinterfaces List and Set.

Central to the Spliterator interface are these three methods:

```
Spliterator<T> trySplit ();

default void forEachRemaining (Consumer<? super T> action) {…}

boolean tryAdvance (Consumer<? super T> action);
```

The method trySplit() partitions the underlying data in two. It creates a new Spliterator with half the data and keeps the other half in the original instance. Each can be given to a thread which, in turn, iterates over the partitioned data using forEachRemaining(). The method tryAdvance() is a one-at-a-time variant that returns the next element or null if the list has been exhausted.

Spliterators do not handle parallel processing themselves but provide the abstraction to do so. Here's the concept in action:

```
public static boolean isMovieInList(String title, List<String> movieList)
    throws InterruptedException {
    // Obtain a spliterator from the movie list
    Spliterator<String> s1 = movieList.spliterator ();

    // Split the original list in half.
    // Now s1 and s2 each contains half the list.
    Spliterator<String> s2 = s1.trySplit ();

    BooleanHolder booleanHolder = new BooleanHolder();
    if (s2 != null) {
        Consumer<String> finder =
            movie -> {if (movie.equals(title)) booleanHolder.isFound = true;};

        // Each thread searches the movie list in parallel
        Thread t1 = new Thread(() -> s1.forEachRemaining (finder));
        Thread t2 = new Thread(() -> s2.forEachRemaining (finder));

        t1.start();
        t2.start();
        t1.join();
        t2.join();
    }

    return booleanHolder.isFound;
}

private static class BooleanHolder {
    public boolean isFound = false;
}
```

Given a title and a list of movies, the method isMovieInList() parallelizes the search to determine if it is contained in the list. It sets the flag in booleanHolder to true if found. It obtains a Spliterator instance from the list, splits it in half, and handsoff one half to each thread. The splitting process can be repeated if further threads are available.

Spliterators can be obtained from other Collection types as well as other libraries in the JDK. There are many implementations designed that deal with different characteristics, including finite/infinite, ordered/non-ordered, sorted/non-sorted, and mutable/immutable. They inherit the qualities of their underlying data structure.

Spliterators are a lower-level abstraction designed to give you more fine-grained control over parallelized iteration. However, the API lacks some of the refinements needed to implement functionally-friendly algorithms. In the above example, we needed to store the state in the BooleanHolder for the search.

Wrap up

This completes our overview of the new and improved Java 8 Collections library as well as the standard functional interfaces. Just as there have been many changes in the standard JDK libraries to support functional concepts, expect major changes from 3rd party APIs. But the biggest change is yet to come.

Key points

The new package java.util.function contains a set of functional interfaces. These are grouped into four families, each represented by their archetypes: Consumer, Function, Predicate, and Supplier.

Each family of functional interfaces defines variants that specialize in types and arity.

Functional interfaces also define methods that enable functional composition. Multiple disparate lambdas can be fused to form super functions that appear as one.

The Collections library has been revamped and functionalized. This has been achieved using default methods at top levels of the hierarchy, thereby ensuring backward compatibility.

The new functional methods in Collections, Lists, Sets, and Maps have been designed with internal iteration in mind. Behavioral parameters in the form of lambdas and method references are given to methods that iterate over collections and act upon each element.

An internal iteration is a form of declarative programming that is fundamental to functional programming. It relieves the developer from having to describe the "how" to do it and focuses instead on the "what" to do.

Spliterators are designed for parallel iteration over collections. Data is partitioned, and each chunk is handed to different threads for parallel processing.

A number is greater than one that is not prime.

CONCLUSION

The JDK is the Java Development Kit, and it is a necessary tool required for compiling, documenting, and packaging Java programs. Together with JRE, an interpreter or loader is built-into the JDK, a compiler called javac, an archiver (JAR), the Javadoc document generator, and many other tools required for successful Java development.

The JRE is the Java Runtime Environment. It is the environment in which the Java bytecode may be executed, and it is used for implementing the Java Virtual Machine. The JRE also provides us with all the class libraries and many other support files required at runtime by the JVM. It is, in basic terms, a software package that provides us with everything we need for running Java programs, a physical implementation of the Java Virtual machine.

JVM stands for Java Virtual Machine. The JVM is an abstract machine, a specification that provides us with the JRE in which our bytecode is executed. The

JVM must follow these notations— Specification, which is a document describing how the JVM is implemented, Implementation, which is a program meeting the JVM specification requirements, and Runtime Instance, which is the JVM instance that gets created whenever the command prompt is used to write a Java command and run a class.

All three are inextricably linked, and each relies on the others to work.

With this, I would like to thank you for choosing my guide on Java programming. As you can see, it is a simple yet complex language, with so many different aspects to learn. By now, you should have a good understanding of the core concepts of Java programming and how to use it.

Your next step is, quite simply, practice. And keep on practicing. You cannot possibly read this guide once and think that you know it all. I urge you to take your time going through this; follow the tutorials carefully and don't move on from any section until you fully understand it and what it all means.

To help you out, there are several useful Java forums to be found online, full of people ready, and willing to help you out and point you in the right direction. There are also loads of online courses, some free and some that you need to pay for, but all of them are useful and can help you take your learning to the next level.

Did you enjoy this guide? I hope that it was all you wanted and more, and it has put you on the right path to getting your dream job!

I hope that you found my introduction to computer programming helpful. It's a very basic start, but it should have given you some idea as to how to begin. It should also have shown you that computer programming really isn't all that difficult and can be quite exciting, especially as you start to see your results appear on the screen and see your computer, in short, doing what it's told to do!

If you found that this has given you a good idea of what to expect, then you may want to move on to more advanced programming in your chosen language. A word of warning here: don't try to learn more than one language at a time; otherwise, you'll find yourself in a muddle. The only other piece of advice I will give you at this stage is to practice... and keep on practicing. The more you do, the more you'll learn, and the more you'll want to learn.

Thank you for downloading my book; if you found it helpful, please consider leaving me a review at Amazon.com.